I0391026

# More Thoughts

# on

# Leadership

...Together with *Thoughts on Leadership,*
**The Definitive Guides**

on Management and Leadership

John P. McWilliams

More Thoughts On Leadership

Copyright 2017
By John P. McWilliams


First printing: November 2017

**Reservation of Rights**

    All rights reserved. No part of this publication may be reproduced or transmitted in any form or by any means, electronic or mechanical, including photocopying, recording, or any information storage and retrieval system, without the express written permission from the author and/or the publisher.


ISBN-13: 978-1541341593 (CreateSpace-Assigned)
ISBN-10: 1541341597



Tel.: (866) 356-2153
Website: www.createspace.com

*Printed in the United States of America*

# Disclaimer

The Publisher, CreateSpace (Amazon), and the author hereby exclude all liability to the extent permitted by the law for any errors or omissions, or opinions expressed in this book and for any loss, damage or expense (whether direct or indirect) suffered by a third party relying on any information contained in the text or within illustrations, or photographs contained in this book.

# Dedication

I dedicate this book to all Leaders. Their burdens are seldom realized by their followers.

"Great corporate leaders are bold, self-assured and know what they don't know, but they hire those who do know...to fill the void."

- John P. McWilliams

# Other Works[1,2] By The Same Author

## Non-Fiction

New Mexico: A Glimpse Into An Enchanted Land
(Out of Print - send an email to author at:
2braveharts@gmail.com)

Against the Wind: Courageous Apache Women[1,2]

## Poetry/Poetic Memoir

Days of Innocence (Poetic Memoir)[1]

Ramblings (Poetry)[1]

## Management/Leadership

Thoughts on Leadership

## Short Stories- Fiction

Santa's Favorite Christmas Tales[1]

Oh Billy, Billy...We Hardly Knew Ya[1]

## Scottish Folktales

Selected Scottish Tales -
Retold by the Story - Teller

[1]  See www.amazon.com for purchase
[2]  See www.barnesandnoble.com for purchase

# Table of Contents

# Table of Contents - Continued

# Acknowledgments

I wish to acknowledge all my many mentors in my lifetime for their guidance, shared experience and wisdom! I'd never have learned about leadership and management but for their wonderful direction and fine example.

One truly learns from one's own mistakes and from the mistakes of others. As I have stated many times: "We learn more from our mistakes and failures than from our successes. Sad but true."

The Author

More Thoughts On Leadership

# Preface

Since I first published *Thoughts on Leadership*, I found that much remained to be said that was not contained in the previous book. This book is the result of those contemplations. The emphasis remains pragmatic: readability, informability, enjoyability and comprehension. The emphasis is on practice, not theory. My hope, as before, is that many of these additional thoughts can be and will be passed along to a new and budding breed of managers and leaders. The thoughts and guidance contained herein are no less important or valuable than those presented in the first book, *Thoughts on Leadership*. Instead, they should be seen as an augmentation of what has been said before.

Some of these thoughts have occurred as a result of my 38-year engineering/management experience, and some have been either acquired or reinforced as a result of Retail experience gained in more recent years.

A brief biography of the author is presented at the end of this book.

I truly hope that all new readers will find this additional information useful and effective in ensuring the success of their own assignments. Please enjoy!

The Author

More Thoughts On Leadership

# Introduction

# Introduction

*Thoughts on Leadership.* the previous book, was published some time ago. Little has changed. The anecdotes, lessons and comments mentioned there still apply. However, in this follow-on book, I have added some additional thoughts on the topic of 'leadership'. Without 'effective leadership' and a great 'team' to lead not much good can happen.

'Effective leadership" is still very, very important. Notice that I say 'effective' leadership. This is essential. 'Ineffective' experience or leadership that goes in the wrong direction is worthless and may even be counterproductive.

There are many examples in today's world of so-called 'experienced' people. However, I claim that 'experience' must not stand alone. Instead, it must produce positive results. Otherwise, it is an exercise in futility and it is just 'busy' work. In other words, it must be 'effective'. It is not what (s)he says one can do, but what one has proven one can do, that matters. Without demonstrably being effective and efficient, 'leadership' is merely a demonstration that perhaps the individual is merely 'doing' things incorrectly for all that elapsed time. This is useless and counter-productive. It is an illusion. Many people can be fooled by the wealth of so-called experience mentioned by such deceivers of self and others. There is good, effective experience and there is bad, ineffective experience. I vote for the former...always!

Certain 'leads' often can become a supervisor or manager, but is that the 'right' person for the job? Maybe not. Excellent performance at one level lower does not necessarily mean that the chosen employee is ready or even

3

competent enough to manage other 'staff'. The chosen employee must be able to not only demonstrate technical or 'on the job' practical experience. This 'staff' person, who is now responsible for the output of others, must be a 'people' person, and (s)he must understand what motivates or demotivates the people reporting to him or her. It is also necessary to have a properly skilled and motivated 'team' or 'staff' to work with.

To elucidate further, an 'effective' leader, supervisor, manager, director has to have the 'right' personality and may require additional and on-going training in 'people skills' development, not technical implementation skills.

This book too is in no way exhaustive. Nor was the previous one. There is no way in these two books to cover every aspect of 'leadership. They are not meant to be total and comprehensive. Hopefully, they will add to the literature that already exists on this matter.

Many books have been written about the very topics I have and have not discussed here. My hope is that this additional short book will further encourage others to embrace leadership, in any form. It is difficult, yes, but it can also be extremely rewarding and satisfying. I really hope that the 'motivated' will read these discussions and find that they have 'what it takes', that they have the 'right stuff', as they say, to become effective leaders. Remember this: "If something scares you to death, do NOT run away from it, but embrace it instead and run TOWARDS it. Only then will you grow as an individual, and consequently do what others fear to do, and in the process you will overcome any fears you may have."

My intention here is to pass on to another generation lessons learned from my own experiebnce in both the development and the retail spaces. Hopefully, those whe wish to learn some 'leadership' skills will consult either or both of these two books: *Thoughts on Leadership*, the previous publication, or this more recent publication, *More Thoughts on Leadership*.

Good luck to all 'leaders'!

# Chapter One:

# A Leader

# As A

# Facilitator

More Thoughts On Leadership

# Chapter One: A 'Leader' As A Facilitator

A supervisor, manager or 'leader' of any kind has many, many responsibilities. However, since staff is hired to do specific jobs or functions, in order that the overall vision of the 'leader' is implemented, this same staff must be provided with the tools, services, resources and training necessary to do their jobs effectively and efficiently. If these are not provided or if they are provided inadequately, the 'team' or 'staff' will flounder, become ineffective, and waste time trying to do their job (in some less desirable or time-consuming way). Since 'time is money' this is a very ineffective way of doing things. It is better to spend the small amount of money required to enable them to work more efficiently and more effectively!

So, the question is: what does one mean by being a facilitator and what does one do to accommodate this feature? First, it depends upon the type of job or function. What applies in one case may not be required in a different case, but basically it boils down to providing the employee with the facilities, hardware, software, internet access, e-mail access (with necessary restrictions to avoid misuse or abuse), floor space, desks, equipment, tools or supplies, etc, necessary to do their job in the most efficient and effective manner possible.

Second, it can also depend on the skill set or experience set of the employee or employees. Some employees have encountered similar situations before and may be aware of easy and even inexpensive 'work-arounds'. These should be encouraged and be brought to the attention of the supervisor or manager, at the earliest possible opportunity - by the knowing employee. Further, if such 'work-arounds' are later implemented the credit should be given publicly to the suggesting employee, to give credit where it is due, and simultaneously, to encourage others to do so.

Also, experienced employees may already possess the 'know-how' or the 'needed' tools to complete a task. It may not be necessary to provide them with what is needed, only those who lack that know-how or tool.

Some employees also are aware of the most advanced and most recent versions of software, applications, and other tools or methods that may be better suited for the task at hand. Do not be afraid to access this knowledge by approaching that employee for suggestions and ideas. No one loses, when everyone wins.

Another less-observed consequence of not 'facilitating' the employees' needs to complete their job function is the loss of time or monetary value. Besides, there is the immeasurable loss in team morale. If the team sees that the person-in-chief (PIC) is unreceptive to suggestions that make their job do-able or easier, especially for a small monetary investment, there exists the very real possibility that word will spread and future 'worthwhile' suggestions or ideas for improvement will be side-lined or abandoned. This is the 'nail of death' to any successful effort, because the team will feel alienated. Then it will no longer matter what is mandated or suggested by the 'leader'. Ears will close and no message will penetrate. All efforts at improvement will face disaster and failure from that point forward, because the 'team' or 'staff' will have tuned out.

This is especially true of the most motivated and most diligent employees. Those who are less so, will just continue along as before, because they really don't care enough 'to get involved' to begin with. The motivated and diligent may seek the lower ground and basically join the ranks of the 'uncaring', or they will leave and seek employment elsewhere. By so doing, the 'disgruntled employee' may belief that s(he) will then be working for another employer who listens and acts for the employee's benefit. What they really want is to take pride in their job, their workplace and most importantly, in their own contribution and skills. Money, by itself, is a poor and temporary motivator. Job satisfaction and high morale are actually more important and longer lasting as motivators.

If productive employees are not allowed to flourish, because of inadequate tools, facilities or training, or because the 'team' or 'staff' are disabled from performing their task. They will see their efforts as in vain and pointless. So, why bother?

This type of malaise is exactly what a good effective 'leader' tries to avoid and one way to do so is to become the employee team's facilitator or enabler, with respect to doing their assigned tasks. Enabling can be a negative when it 'enables' negative behavior, but not if enabling allows the employee to do or to better do his task. In that case, 'enabling' can be very, very positive and reinforcing.

Demotivating a motivated or diligent employee, means that the average performance of the whole team declines and diminishes - the opposite of what is desired.

Bottom Line: One of a 'leader's' jobs is to empower his employees to do what they do best. This is achieved by being a 'faciltator'. Motivate. Do NOT Demotivate.

Remember: Material costs  are far less than lost labor time costs! Always choose lower labor costs over lower material and resource costs....always!

# More Thoughts On Leadership

Chapter Two:

Encourage Debate & Promote

Diversity of Opinion

More Thoughts On Leadership

# Encourage Debate & Promote
# Diversity of Opinion

Often, debate and adverserial discussion can be looked upon negatively, or even as an indirect or direct challenge to a 'leader's' authority. However, to a strong, experienced and self-assured 'leader', this is the wrong reaction to take under these circumstances.

Instead, the confident and experienced 'leader' will see this as an opportunity to discuss observations and new ideas 'outside the box'. Different and sometimes unique and refreshing perspectives can then be discussed to the benefit of all. It allows one to see situations from an entirely valid and often realistic but different viewpoint...one that has not been considered before. The 'honest leader' will recognize that (s)he cannot 'see' or 'know' everything. To be so gifted would also carry with it an awesome, almost overwhelming responsibility.

So, to be totally realistic and to garner the respect of one's 'team'/'staff', they should be allowed to bring forth new fresh ideas and suggestions. It is wise to encourage, not discourage debate and diversity of opinion. After all, if everyone holds the same point of view, or if debate is discouraged, then, there is no transfer of information and no new knowledge will be forthcoming. The 'team'/'staff' will assume that the same 'tired, old' perspective only will be proclaimed. They will 'tune-out' and listen no longer, because they will come to realize that only one viewpoint is acceptable, and no other.

Diversity of opinion reveals new and sometimes refreshing and exciting avenues of thought. Therefore, since the 'leader' cannot be everywhere or all-knowing, this type of debate ought to be seen as a necessary ingredient to success, as opposed to a threat.

Further, 'self-confident' 'leaders' will seek out others who are not 'yes-men or women' to be placed in positions of responsibility and authority. Only then can the 'leaders' be assured of 'honesty' and forward progress. Never be afraid to bring someone on-board who seeks your position. He or she will work extra hard to get it. In the meantime, an observant 'leader' will notice their desires. Utilize them to the 'leader's' own advantage. Then the 'leader' gains advantage from the efforts of the ambitious and diligent ones. They too will win because the conscientious 'leader' will recognize and reward their efforts accordingly. Everyone wins in this scenario, but it requires the 'leader' to be vigilant at all times.

As an example, as a Director, and before that, as a Department Manager, in a high-tech, Silicon-Valley development company, the out-performers were always sought out. Oftentimes, they so wanted my position that they'd work extra hard to achieve the necessary recognition and 'kudos'. Meanwhile, since they reported to me as the 'leader', the 'leader' (I) was the one to grant that recognition, and simultaneously to reap the benefits of their untiring effort, while they get the recognition that they so covet.

However, to do this successfully, the 'leader' must always be vigilant. It requires skilled observation on the part of that same 'leader'. Otherwise, the 'leader' can be left behind by those same 'outperformers'. Remember, as in the previous chapter, the 'leader' must serve as a 'vigilant enabler', in order to keep the focus on his or her own accomplishments, while reaping all the benefits of the extra effort by the motivated employees. Encouragement and vigilance are the keys.

Never discourage an opinion that is sincerely offered even when it is in conflict with your own perspective. The employee may be capable of seeing or hearing things that you, as the 'leader,' may not. The 'CYA' instinct is very strong. It is really about survival and self-preservation. No one wishes to look like a fool in front of anyone, especially the 'leader'.

As a project 'leader' on one very large development project ($100 milllion) I was encouraged (very strongly) by the Prime Contractor to allow one of their own 'staff' to attend our weekly status meetings. I was assigned to improve team morale and productivity, because morale had plummeted due to Prime Comtractor and Corporate intervention and re-direction of low-level 'staff'. The entire technical team had developed an innate dislike and disrespect for this particular Prime Contractor and even for upper management because of this. There had been a severe erosion of trust and confidence in both the customer (Prime Contractor) and upper-level management, who were 'micro-managing' the project and interfering. To put it more plainly, they loathed each other. The 'team' had been successfullly alienated because of these actions.

The 'team' saw the Prime Contractor representatives as 'stool-pigeons', who'd report back to their own management the day-to-day affairs and status of each subtask, and point fingers. It is known that the customer is always right, as stated in a later chapter. However, this is only true if the customer, in this case the Prime Contractor, is not interfering with 'real' progress or, in any way, re-directing the 'staff' that should be directed by the 'corporate 'leader' only. These Prime Contractor representatives were also seen by the 'team' as obstructive, interruptive and misdirecting. An experienced senior project manager was identified and assigned to clean up this 'mess'. The senior project 'leader' set himself up as the primary interface between the 'staff', the Prime Contractor and Corporate management. This allowed a more even flow of information and direction, because there was always only one person to coordinate with.

The Prime Contractor representatives were disallowed from attending weekly meetings, as they repeatedly requested, because of the obvious CYA'ing and natural dishonesty that would occur among the 'staff' in such a situation, disabling the senior project manager from correcting the 'team' morale. The customer (Prime Contractor) was, however, permitted to participate in the several design reviews and test reviews that occurred in a normal development project. This combination allowed the Customer to provide the proper technical input on design and test while the senior 'leader' was able to eventually improve 'team'/'staff' morale significantly.

The senior project manager, and this is very important, encouraged honesty and difference of opinion to be expressed among the 'staff', not only at the weekly meeting but at any time. That was the only way to gain the respect of the 'staff' and improve the sagging morale issue.

It is very important to listen to peers and to one's 'staff', and to act on any recommendations that are appropriate and accurate. However, it is also important to investigate, verify, if needed, and report back to the 'team' one's findings, pro or con. That way the 'team' does not feel disenfranchised or alienated. 'Be firm but fair', at all times.

This will be quickly grasped by the 'staff', honesty will reign and respect of the 'team' for the 'leader' will accrue. They will quickly see, even if unimplemented by the 'leader', that their perspective, comments and suggestions are worthy of consideration by the 'leadership'. This can only help to improve team morale and assist in the 'team-building' process. By implementing such an approach the 'leader' has a better chance of achieving his or her stated mission or objectives. All will feel that they are an important part of the 'team'.

In time, this and many other changes allowed the morale to re-surge, but a big part of it was the ability, that was encouraged, to be honest, to express a difference of opinion, and to 'tell it like it really is', not what one wants to hear but what really and actually was happening.

In this way, any problems can be properly addressed in a timely and effective manner. In the end, the 'leader', the 'team' and all associated with the 'team' effort will benefit. In this particular case, although the Prime Contractor would never admit it, they too benefitted from more realistic schedules, prioritization and forward progress. There were no losers...only winners!

Bottom Line: Rise above the fray and accept other, sometimes opposing arguments, offered in good faith. Encourage debate and controversy. The results can truly be stunning. If the comments are indeed constructive, the benefits can far outweigh the time or money spent considering them. Improvements in efficacy and efficiency may flourish.

Most employees respond very positively to this kind of openness and acceptance on the part of a 'leader'. They most often want to be part of any improvement. Allow them to do so, with the appropriate follow-thru and filtering. A 'true' 'leader 'will never be sorry.

More Thoughts On Leadership

**Chapter Three:**

**A 'Leader' Needs**

**To Get His or Her Act Together**

**Before and After Any Meeting**

More Thoughts On Leadership

## Chapter Three: A 'Leader Needs To Get His or Her Act Together Before and After Any Meeting

Organization is a key to success. However, here I wish not to talk about organizational structure. No, instead, here I wish to discuss how a 'leader' needs to personally organize, or 'get his or her act together' prior to and immediately following a meeting. This is still organization but it is on a personal level, as opposed to a corporate level.

The team always needs to know what the 'leader' has in mind, in order to allow proper execution of the 'leader's' goals. Without knowing what the daily or weekly, or even longer expectations are, this is difficult to achieve. The 'staff'/'team' need to remember and refer back to what was discussed and agreed upon at any group meeting. This is also true of the 'leader'. The only realistic and lasting way to do that is to document everything, by writing it down, for future reference, for all to see and comment, if necessary.

For example, every formal meeting or 'get-together' ought to be preceded by a meeting agenda, so that every 'staff' member knows the purpose of the meeting, what is to be discussed, and what is to be done, both short term and long term. By being so prepared and informed each 'staff' member can be prepared for the upcoming meeting. This requires more effort on the part of the 'leader' but it is well-worth it! The benefits accrued can be spectacular because the 'staff' or 'team' is well-organized and always knows what is expected of them.

In addition, all affected 'leaders' should attend these

23

meetings to present a uniformed and united front, and for future enforcement and follow-through. It is unwise not to have all such sub-'leaders' attend. If they do not show up, the 'staff' will notice and come to the conclusion that the issues discussed are not that important to the missing sub-leader. Lateness by anyone should never be tolerated, unless extenuating circumstances exist. It sets a poor example, for all to see.

An additional need at every meeting is that of taking and publishing the 'minutes' of the meeting. Again, the purpose here is to document all comments made and decisions agreed upon, in written form for future reference by all attendees, and even by those who were unable to attend for whatever reason. Usually, such minutes are recorded by a secretary or some other administrator. If this is not feasible or practical then someone else can be assigned to perform this important function.

In any case, Minutes of the Meeting ought to be published and made available to all staff within 24 hours of the meeting's end. Minutes need also to include any Action Items that have been assigned during the meeting. This way, every 'staff' member knows his or her assigned responsibiliy, the assigned priority, due date, etc.

One might ask, why is it iso mportant to document each meeting in a written manner? With ten people attending any meeting, there will be ten different interpretations of the issues discussed, the priority assigned, the due date, the assignee, the agreements reached, etc. It is therefore necessary to 'normalize' all this confusion by having the 'leader' or his or her documentor issue the Minutes, under the 'leader's' name, after the 'leader' has reviewed the Minutes document for accuracy. In this way, there is only one interpretation that counts and that is the published 'leader's' account of the meeting, in the Minutes. By publishing ther Minutes, however, any disagreemt or misinterpretation can be quickly resolved and the clarified or corrected Minutes redistributed, if necessary.

From the 'leader's' perspective, it is paramount that all 'staff' members see the outcome of the meeting in the same light, to ensure that the 'team' is correctly aligned to achieve the 'leader's' goals and objectives. Different interpretations of the meeting only leads to chaos and confusion. It also leads to forgetfulness, and diminishes the chance of proper execution and implementation. If Minutes are not generated, and the 'staff' forgets what was agreed upon, which is highly likely, then the possibility of revisiting the same topic is also highly likely, with the commensurate loss of time and efficiency. This is very undesirable and leads to repetition and lack of 'follow-through'.

Bottom Line: "The 'leader' gets outs what the 'leader' puts in, or as is commonly stated, 'garbage in, garbage out'.

The more personally organized the 'leader', the more items are documented, written down. published and understood, the more productive the 'team' can be expected to be, and the greater the likelihood of achieving the company's or the project goals.

More Thoughts On Leadership

# Chapter Four:

# Supervisors: the First Line of

# Management & Leadership -

# Who, What and How

More Thoughts On Leadership

# Chapter Four: Supervisors: The First Line of Management & Leadership - Who, What and How

Supervisors usually are the first line of management or of leadership. So, the begging question becomes: Who should be chosen for this first position of managerial authority, responsibility and accountability?

Usually the preceding role of such a candidate is a lead of some kind. However, a lead often has little or no real authority over others. He or she may provide input, and give daily direction about the work that is required and who it may best be assigned to, from a day-to-day perspective. In this sense, the role is largely technical or job-related. It is usually someone who is skilled, experienced and senior in that particular field. He or she is usually knowledgeable about what is required to do a given task, and is skilled at doing that same task himself or herself.

However, being a supervisior is one level above a 'lead' and it usually requires that the candidate possess not only the day-to-day technical or 'on the job' skills and experience, but also indefinable but obvious 'people skills'. In other words, the candidate should be good with people, This requires a much different skill set from what is required below this leadership role or level. It requires a certain level of intangible skill in handling and assigning individuals to a task. It requires a certain level of sensitivity to the needs of others, a knowledge of each individual's motivation and skill level, as well as their often-complex personal issues. It requires a certain timely level of firmness and understanding.

It requires flexibility and a firm base of knowledge in body language and being able to 'read' people. It also requires a knowledge, obtained or obtainable, of the corporate personnel rules. This position as well as other managerial positions, require the ability not only to 'read' people, and to discern their real needs (for the job), but it also requires the ability to 'listen'. Not everyone is a good listener, technically capable or not.

In addition, it requires a keen eye to see what others may not see or be capable of seeing in the individual. An individual may not follow the letter of the corporate rules in every regard but may otherwise be very diligent, and possess a self-directed and highly motivated work-ethic. Instead of scolding these same individuals it may be better to praise them for their other worthy efforts while instructing them in the areas of which they may not even be aware. This prevents unnecessary alienation of the most diligent and motivated employeses over an issue that may not be that important in the long run.

Not every excellent technical or skilled individual makes a 'good' supervisor. The requirements are very different and should be recognized by the top 'leader'. Some fail miserably, because of the very different skill set required of them. Some, possess a natural ability to make the proper adjustment. Such individuals may,. by personality, possess the necessary 'people skills'. In addition, such individuals may openly accept additional 'personal' training to improve their 'people skills.' Some may never do so. It is up to the top manager or 'leader' to be discerning enough to be able to tell the difference.

The next question to be answered is: What does a supervisor do? Not only does a supervisor coordinate the day-to-day activities of the assigned task(s), he or she must become familiar with the corporate Human Resource (HR) rules, as well as the quirks of each employee assigned under that supervisor.

There is another role of the supervisor that is less obvious. That role or function is to help reduce the workload of the ranks higher up in the leadership chain. After all, such higher-level management individuals usually have more than enough to accomplish on a daily basis. They bear a great many responsibilities on their shoulders. The supervisor can help to relieve that burden somewhat, by properly directing lower level staff. By making appropriate decisions that relieve the higher level leaders from having to address trivial matters, allows them the time to make the necessary stategic decisions. It should not be necessary to bother the higher level leader with mundane, trivial issues that a properly-groomed lead person or even a supervisor could easily answer. The lower the decision level the better ...it is for the efficacy of the organization, This reduces the need for a deep vertical organization, and for a massive, unnecessary bureaucracy. It empowers the individual staff member.

The last significant question is: How does a supervisor go about his or her job? The How is implemented by following many of the suggestions mentioned above and by being knowledgeable, 'people sensitive', supportive of the top level leadership without overburdening them, and by being able to correctly interpret upper management's general strategic directives at the day-to-day tactical level. Alienation is counter-productive and generally will lead to diligent, motivated individuals leaving or otherwise 'tuning out'. This should always be avoided where possible.

The supervisor can also aid in defining staffing needs to the upper leadership. No team can properly do its job if it is under-staffed, regardless of the leadership, but it is up to the 'leader' to adequately define any staffing shortages.

Supervisors can also, based upon input from the supervisors' staff, identify unnecessary duplications in assignments, in approaches, in inventory, etc. These must be eliminated to positively affect efficiency and to have any possibilty of achieving project or company goals.

Non-performance should never be tolerated. It depresses morale and it sets a bad example for others. This is often one role that the supervisor must execute successfully in order for the organization to meet its objectives. The supervisor should be in a position to see such non-performance and to identify this to the upper leadership (but only if absolutely necessary and uncorrectable at the supervisor's level), and to create the necessary back-up documentation, when needed. Such a non-performing staff member  needs to be warned, first verbally, and if the condition persists, by written documentation. This creates a documented 'track record' that avoids any legal issues from arising later on.  It also awards the employee the opportunity to take his or her own corrective action without any further warning from the supervisor. Termination may result if the individual takes no responsibility for his or her non-performance and does nothing to change the situation. This is always unpleasant for any supervisor or manager but sometimes it is necessary. Unlikable though termination of an employee may be, it is also a supervisor's  responsibility and part of his or her job function.

If a supervisor can be successful in these regards, he or she will eventually be able to join higher leadership positions within the organization.

The bottom line: Develop 'people skills' at every opportunity. Sensitivity and firmness are very important in handling staff to achieve the overall project or corporate goals. These cannot be achieved consistently without knowledge of 'people skills'. The definition of who (should be chosen), what (the position entails) and how (the responsibilities are executed) for a given supervisory role are defined herein.

More Thoughts On Leadership

# Chapter Five:

# Mutual Respect

More Thoughts On Leadership

# Chapter Five: Mutual Respect

Mutual respect is very important and it must be demonstrated 'across the board' and at all levels. It should be demonstrated and shown to everyone: customers, staff, management, and to one another. So what is respect?

It is a manner of behavior and human interaction. It means treating and talking to another individual as you yourself would wish to be addressed. It means, no 'attitude' by any means whatsoever, via e-mail, face-face conversation, phone conversation, direction from 'leaders' to staff, comments from staff to 'leaders', interaction with customers. A positive interaction should always be demonstrated between staff in front of customers, intercom or walkie-talkie interaction, and any other means, both private and public. It means dropping ANY and ALL sarcasm and sarcastic remarks. It means giving deference to another regardless of skill, education or know-how. Most of all it means treating others, higher or lower in position and responsibility, as fellow human beings - not as objects of scorn or dislike.

Without mutual respect there exists a negative tension in the workplace. If respect is lacking between the 'staff' and the 'leadership', one can be certain that the 'leader's' or project's goals and objectives will never be successfully realized. This is common sense.

All individuals want to be treated with due respect. If not, the employee can become alienated, morale of the 'team' can suffer negatively, as word spreads of that individual's negative treatment. The 'leader's' directives can then be ignored, making the ultimate achievement of the project goals so much more difficult to achieve.

If the disrespected employee leaves, then he or she needs to be replaced with another who needs to be informally (OJT) or formally (Training Courses) retrained, both of which are less efficient and will cause a slip in schedule, increased costs and possibly a drop in performance. All of these cause more difficulties in the timely and cost-effective achievement of the larger goals. The main sufferor will be the 'team leader' and the 'team' members as employment or advancement may be negatively impacted and achievement of the corporate goals may become unattainable.

A little bit of courtesy and respect can go a long way towards ultimate goal success.

Remember the staff and the customer see and hear much more than one might think. The best way is to treat everyone in the same respectful way. That way no accidents or slips can occur, inadvertently, and no one can see what doesn't exist.

How everyone treats one another, especially in front of a customer, can reflect either negatively or positively on the store or on the corporate environment. 'Leaders' should make sure that reflection is positive.

Bottom Line: Disrespect should never be tolerated for any reason, by the 'leadership'. Furthermore, the 'leadership' should set the example, by always being respectful and non-sarcastic in any verbal exchange with anyone. When staff see the 'leadership' doing this, they too will follow the fine example. 'Leadership' establishes the culture of what is acceptable or unacceptable.

Therefore, it is truly up to the 'leadership' to set the desired example of behavior. Make it be respectful and courteous at all times and to everyone.

# Chapter Six:

## 'Praise' and 'Admonishment'

More Thoughts On Leadership

# Chapter Six: 'Praise' & 'Admonishment'

Implementation of praise and admonition require that the 'leader' or 'supervisor' possess experience with handling 'staff' and he or she must demonstrate 'people skills' and a level of human sensitivity. These actions are most often provided by the 'supervisor', but sometimes by the next higher level of task, project or company 'leadership'. The desired goal is to make clear to each and every employee that exemplary behavior and accomplishment is the expected acceptable operating mode. That is not to say that such interaction and achievement should go unacknowledged or unrecognized. Quite the contrary!

'Praise' should always be done in the presence of the staff member's peers. Make the 'praise' very public. The reason is 'to drive the point home' that extraordinary performance is recognized and rewarded.

'Admonition', however, should be done one-on-one, privately and never in front of one' s peers. Make it very private and unembarrassing for the employee...but effective. Take into account what the employee has done correctly and express it to the employee. Show or ask for ways to improve. Stay positive throughout. This is one of the most challenging aspects of 'leadership'.

A publically 'admonished' 'staff' member can become very defensive. In addition, accustations may be false or based on faulty data, and as a result both the 'staff' member and the 'leadership' can become unnecessarily embarrassed by an accusation made in public.

The most significant downfall of 'admonishing' a

'staff' member in public is that it violates the 'survival' rule. It may cause the accused 'staff' member to 'lash-out' against the 'leadership', causing a diminishment in 'team' morale

It may also cause unnecessary and permanent alienation of the 'staff' member, especially if the 'staff' member is otherwise very diligent and motivated or the accusation is either false or trivial. The triviality is certainly not worth the sacrifice or alienation of an otherwise diligent, motivated 'staff' or 'team' member. Especially when other 'staff' members have made more agregious transgressions and those transgressions are not pointed out or recognized by the 'leadership'. This can cause resentment and frustration to flourish. It does not really matter if no names are mentioned because the 'staff' can usually figure out the un-named 'staff' member through context and elimination.

These two topics ought not to receive equal treatment or be handled in the same identical manner by any kind of 'leader'. Individual recognition, by itself, goes a long way towards raising the morale of the recognized individual(s) but it also does the same for the team. The team then sees that superior performance is not only recognized but oftentimes it is rewarded, with monetary rewards & bonuses, higher raises, increased esteem, letters of commendation from customers, gift cards, recognition awards, etc.

The overall approach should be to 'praise' in public but to 'admonish' in private. Admonishment is by its nature 'negative' and ought to be handled in a private face-to-face way only.

However, the 'leadership' should not only rely upon customer commendations as input for this type of praise. The 'leadership' should determine its own assessment of each worker and 'staff' member. This is done  by careful observation of the work habits, demonstrated 'people skills', out-performance of individual 'staff' members, organizational skills, high diligence and motivation levels, great initiative shown by its 'staff' members, etc. Such assessment can then be augmented as required by customer commendations to form a true and independent picture of every 'staff' member on the 'team'.

The flaw in only regarding customer commendations, in a retail environment, lies in the observation that women are more likely to take the time to write to the corporate management than is a man. Most men will not do this.

This is not a sexist statement but merely an observational fact. Therefore the 'staff' member who has some very positive interaction with male customers may not be fairly represented. Independent assessment by the internal 'leadership' can compensate for this inadvertent bias. Thi should always be done regardkless of gender, for it is the only way to derive a balanced abnd fair assessment of each employee.

The Bottom Line: 'Praise' in public but 'Admonish' in private. The 'team' or the 'staff' are best served that way, and alienation is seldom a result.

More Thoughts On Leadership

**Chapter Seven:**

**One Needs To Know Where One Is Going**

**& How To Get There**

# More Thoughts On Leadership

# Chapter Seven: One Needs To Know Where One Is Going & How To Get There

Ever try to go somewhere but you have no GPS or map to guide you? Hard to do, unless you have been there before and you already know the way. For anything new, it is almost impossible to find your way correctly to the desired end-point.

The same is true of one's career. Not only does one need to know where one is going, but one needs to know how to get there, and how well (or not) one is doing on the current position.

There are several elements required to solve this problem: 1. a properly detailed job description; 2. requirements to fulfill and responsibilities of the new position; 3. a schedule of performance reviews/salary increases: when and where they will occur.

The Job Description is exactly what it sounds like. It describes the requirements to obtain the job position, in terms of skills, capabilities, seniority and education. It defines the responsibilities and job function of the position. It indicates to the job seeker what skills, or education or equivalent he or she must possess to fulfill the position. For those who already hold the position, it defines his or her job function and associated responsibilities. The Job Description may or may not define the salary range of that position. Different companies handle this in different ways. The Job Description often describes the level, or the limits of the authority granted to the holder of the job described.

47

The second item mentioned above is often but not always defined in the Job Description. If not, then the requirements defined for the position are separately defined. Either way, the applicant knows exactly what is expected of the job seeker at each position. In this sense, a road map is provided for future career development.

A 'staff' member needs to know when various performance and salary adjustment reviews are to be held and where, in advance. Is it at the 6-month point, or the yearly anniversary? Is it different, depending upon seniority? What is the average percentage raise at each of those times, among one's peers? By so knowing one can gauge oneself against others. One cannot plan or work out a path to 'leadership' if one does not possess the necessary skills, or can't obtain them through the proper training. It is necessary to know the requirements and responsibilities of each position along the way. If one has no idea of when any job reviews take place, and under what circumstances, then there is no feedback and the 'staff' member is blinded. Also, the progressing or advancing 'staff' member then has no sense of how he or she is doing in the current position relative to his or her peers, because there has been no feedback from upper management.

Bottom Line: It comes down to knowledge. In this case, it is knowledge about how one gets to where one is hopefully going, along with knowledge of the requirements of the position one wishes to obtain. Hard work and a good work ethic, by themselves, are helpful and necessary but not sufficient. One needs to know what is required to obtain the necessary credentials or education, and to prepare for the challenges ahead. It is very difficult, if not impossible to do this, without knowledge of how to get to your career destination. These elements help to provide a road map of how to get there.

# Chapter Eight:

## Formality Can Be A Good Thing

More Thoughts On Leadership

# Chapter Eight: Formality Can Be A Good Thing

Formality can be an organizational tool if properly applied. For example, it is a good thing to assign a head to every department in the organization, to assign reponsibilities and to hold the assigned individuals accountable for their decisions and their actions.

It is also a good idea, to formalize the exchange of information between these department heads and the upper leadership. How so?

First, there ought to be one department head, supervisor or manager for each department. That individual then becomes responsible for the daily work assignments of each staff member under his or her jurisdiction. He or she also becomes responsible for any theft in that department, if the entity is a retail store, or for missing (stolen) equipment or software in a development environment. In a development organization, such reponsibility can be asssigned to a Lab Manager (for physical equipment and test gear). In most companies, computers, and associated software, can be assigned to an internal IT person. Office furniture and the like can be assigned to a departmental facilities person. The assigned 'staff' member or 'leader', asssigned to overlook this equipment must also develop a plan to reduce abuses.

However, formality can be painful because it requires a level of documentation that many find burdensome or unnecessary. This formal documentation serves as the 'corporate' or 'team' memory.

It is also desirable to require that a weekly written

report be generated and submitted to the next higher managemnt or 'leadership' level, with a pre-defined format, from each department head. It must be written on a regular basis and distributed to at least one's junior leaders and to the senior staff, if it exists. It is also useful to include the next higher level of management on the distribution list. This allows written and documented feedback from the lead, department head or junior mangement to the top 'leadership' or management levels, so that upper management support or follow-through (correction) can occur. It informs them on a regular basis of progress and issues.

Such a format should define (a). accomplishments and achievements or progress against a pre-defined plan, (b). identifies problems or issues including departmental suggestions or proposed solutions to the identified problems. This serves as a documented communication vehicle that, if acted upon and adequately supported, can bring about immediate solutions to many identified issues and problems. Without the proper, regular documentation and reporting, such issues may otherwise remain un-identified, and linger without solution. Such non-identification can mean that the problems persist and therefore will continue or increase unabated.

Some problems cannot be solved without upper level support because the problems are systemic in nature. These types of issues or problems are often inter-departmental. They can usually only be resolved at upper levels of management, and require that level of support.

Other issues are purely intra-departmental, and solutions can usually be found within the affected department by the identified department head. In either case, upper management should be made aware of the issue, ensure that all necesary resources are adequately provided. Proposed solutions ought to be encouraged.

Sometimnes, one or more of the identified issue are experienced by more than one department. This is one other reason for the formality of a weekly report and for regular meetings with the assigned department heads or team/staff leads.

Communication and feedback are like the oil used to reduce friction. It allows the various parts to work smoothly and efficiently. Weekly pre-defined reports and regular formalized meetings have the desired effect of increasing the internal level of communication and feedback. Both of these are essential for improved performance and for the identification of timely corrective action.

Bottom Line: The correct amount of formalization can be a very good and necessary thing, if properly implemented. One does not wish to overburden one's head people, but some written formalization can help to produce startling results and timely improvements. These help to ensure ultimate project, task or corporate  success.

The reward: the 'leader'  will be identified as organized,  methodical,  improvement-oriented  and disciplined. Further,  (s)he will be identified as an 'effective' 'leader', who ultimately achieves his or her stated goals and objectives, through a process of constant improvement. This method works, I can assure you.

More Thoughts On Leadership

# Chapter Nine:

# Training

More Thoughts On Leadership

# Chapter Nine: Training

Many staff require some degree of formal training. Some need less than others because they may already possess the required skill set or experience. Others may find formal training to be useful, and of great benefit if he or she is weak or unfamiliar with the methods expostulated in the formal training course. Some others may find such formal training a waste of time. There is nothing, other than admonition and possible firing, that can correct this attitude or behavior.

It is always a good idea for the 'leadership' to maintain a file of a particular employee's training, education or skill set. This way, it is easily known what still may be required for any particular employee in the way of training, formal or informal, to continue to excel in his or her current position or to advance to a more senior position.

Of course, the most elemental training is termed On The Job (OTJ) training. This is informal and basically is defined as the day-to-day learning that takes place by the employee. The OJT in a development environment is often very different from what might be required in a retail store. But each may require it...but different needs apply to each situation.

In most any environment, development, retail or other an employee is expected to learn a great deal on his or her own, in order to do the job efficiently and effectively. In my own experience, as a budding development engineer, I taught myself how silicon controlled rectifiers (SCR's) worked, impedance transformations, programming in Fortran, etc. Later I learned other software programming languages. I also had to learn optics and magnetic deflection for an assignment in air-fighter cockpit display design. Not to bore the reader, but these were required of me in order for me to function as a contributing engineer.

In a retail environment the requirements are usually less formal: how to make duplicate keys, the usage or applicability of items in various departments, organization of inventory for ease of restocking, putting stock away in the proper location, working the registers, cleaning up, customer interaction and support, etc. Again, this is 'hands-on' training or OTJ training. It is informal. As opposed to this, there is often the need for additional 'formal' training such as OSHA, or federal employment requirements, safety regulations for handling firearms, various types of welding as well as their application, interpersonnal skills, or management 'people skills', development, body language interpretation, etc.

In a development environment, the need may be in specific disciplines such as DSP (Digital Signal Processing), programming in a specific language and language level, the use of specific software tool or its application, program management methodologies, Earned Value Methods, etc.

In either case, there is an inherent initial investment of time and money required by the company and the employee. This may be perfectly acceptable in lower turn-over situations, such as development, where there is a real chance that the initial investment pays off. However, this may be highly undesirable in higher turn-over situations, such as retail, where the employee may become trained, the cost expended only to find the employee seeking a new job, outside the company. In such cases more formal training should perhaps be reserved for long-time employees or for those in managerial or supervisory positions.

Decisions such as these can only be recommended

by the department heads, but approved by the higher level managers and leaders, for obvious financial reasons. The overall goal is to improve efficiency and effectivity but at a reasonable cost and investment. If there is little chance of a return on the initial investment, why bother? This is the main difference between the development environment and the retail environment. Any 'leader' should be cognizant of this major difference in any decisions that are made. There is only so much budget available in either case. The difference is the potential return that can be expected on that initial investment, and generally the turn-over rate is much higher in an 'unprofessional' environment.

Bottom Line: Training of one sort or another is usually necessary to bring employees up to speed on their task assignments. However, the mix of informal OTJ training and more formalized training is subject to the nature of the job. Informal training may be required of any job type but more formal objectified training may only be required in certain instances where the investment made by the company pays for itself in improved efficiency and productivity. If the formally trained employee, seeks another position in another company shortly after such a costly initial investment on the part of the company, then there is no real point in having the company support such formalized training.

A good manager/'leader' usually knows the difference and acts accordingly.

More Thoughts On Leadership

# Chapter Ten:

# Mandates vs Openness

More Thoughts On Leadership

# Chapter Ten: Mandates vs Openness

There always exists a tension between mandating or commanding the 'staff' and a more flexible, open approach to management and 'leadership'. The truth is there are occasions which arise when the use of one or the other is required. The key is flexibility.

There are times when certain positions or goals must be mandated, because there is no other choice. However, it is always best to get 'buy-in' from the staff. This allows the best chance of achieving the 'leader's' goals. When the 'team' or 'staff' 'buys-in' or supports the cause, it becomes part of them and they will usually move 'heaven and earth' to complete the task properly, on time, and on or under budget. Their own reputation is then on the line and few individuals will allow their own prestige to suffer.

As I stated in the first book, ***Thoughts on Leadership***, it is better to allow the team to come forward with the very idea that is desired rather than to arbitrarily mandate such an outcome. In the previous book, I presented an example from the development environment. If I, as PM or as Director saw that a project was behind schedule, I would point out this deficiency to the assigned employees. I would then inject a 'pregnant' pause as they debated how to address the unfolding issue. Inevitably, the usual response was to volunteer his or her own time on weekends to attempt to restore the original schedule. Rather than mandate that they make up the time, flexibility allowed them to volunteer the same time themselves. It is always better to receive a personal committment from a 'staff' member than to mandate a correction. The 'staff' member usually will then meet or work towards meeting his or her own personal committent. The result is also less resentment on the part of the employee.

The 'staff' in this case may be open to 'overtime' pay or some other incentive. (This may not even be available to the salaried employee.)

Obviously, this would not work the same with non-salaried employees such as those that work in a retail or sales environment. Nonetheless, the basic principle is still the same. However, the financial motivation is achieved differently. The (financial) incentive is usually more immediate in time.

If possible, it is best to allow the 'staff' to identify the solution, rather than have the 'leader' mandate the solution from above. Sometimes, this is impossible to do, and then mandates are the inevitable result, but wherever and whenever possible it is best to be flexible and open to ideas that originate with the 'staff'. Thereby, the requirement is not seen as 'overbearing'.

By doing so, the 'leader' is seen as reasonable and non-intimidating. Flexibility over compulsion is always best, unless there is no other choice. Flexibility results in higher 'team' morale, tighter 'team' spirit and a willingness to work with the 'leader' to achieve the common goal, as defined by the 'leader'. The last thing a true 'leader' wants is to be perceived as a dictator, who is rigid and uncompromising in his or her approach. It is better to be flexible and open to suggestion.

This ties in to an earlier discussion on the need to encourage diversity of opinion. Let the staff define the way to make up any deficiency. The staff usually works closest to the problem at hand and probably possesses an innate undertstanding of how best to address the problem or issue.

A 'leader' must have trust and confidence in his or

her employees. 'Staff' usually come through when given the trust they deserve, but are often not given. They also need to be provided the correct opportunity to properly function. Besides, many staff members become motivated when the 'leader' looks to his or her 'staff' for a solution. They can become charged, as if on a mission. The 'leader' should always encourage such a burst of enthusiasm.

The real key is to get everyone aligned towards solving shared problems. Only the 'leader' can reveal these as he or she has purview over all activities within his or her area of jurisdiction.

Bottom Line: Involve one's staff in the identification of common problems and involve them in the ultimate solution. Pride in their own contribution is a great morale booster and may very well result in the 'leader's' achievement of his or her , or the 'team' or 'corporate' goals and objectives.

Instead of one person trying to solve the problem, the 'leader' thereby involves the efforts of all his or her 'staff', who may very well be very knowledgeable on the issue. The result is always positive and the benefit always accrues to the 'leader', because he or she had the good sense to listen to one's 'staff' instead of pretending that he or she is omniscient, knowing all and everything.

# More Thoughts On Leadership

# Chapter Eleven:

# Customer Interaction

# More Thoughts On Leadership

# Chapter Eleven: Customer Interaction

This is a very important topic. Whether one is involved in a development or a retail environment the main mantras are: 1. Always be courteous, accomodating and helpful to a customer; 2. Try to understand the problem that the customer is trying to solve. Oftentimes, the customer may understand the problem but not know the real solution. This presents an opportunity to work together in solving the problem. In turn, this builds trust and confidence: qualities that can never be bought; 3. Never, ever argue with a customer. It will only cause defensiveness and alienation. You may never see that customer again, because, if nothing else, his or her ego has been bruised. Remember the old adage: 'The customer is always right, even when he is wrong'. In the end, his or her and even your opinion matters not, if the current sale and future sales are lost in the process; 4. Always consider the needs of the customer and act accordingly; 5. Always attempt to build a rapport with a customer. He or she may not buy now but good, positive interaction is usually long-lasting, and the same customer may very well return at some later time, and purchase at that time.

Sometimes establishing such a relationship or rapport seems unproductive at the moment, but it may result in payback at some future date. The other key is to be genuine. Do not fawn or fall all over the customer. Be yourself, within the proper limits of good decorum, but most importantly be true to yourself, be honest, be sincere. Falsities and false behavior can easily be detected. False behavior is one sure way to alienate a customer because he or she does not know what to believe and what not to believe. Trust will quickly vanish under such circumstances.

It is also advisable to never talk politics, or religion with a customer. Such talk may very well alienate a customer, especially if he or she holds an entirely different opinion. So, it is best to avoid these topics at all times.

It is best to stay with the matter at hand, or with the reason the customer is there in the first place. No point in taking an unnecessary risk. The downside is too great and the upside is too uncertain, to attempt to navigate these treacherous waters.

If these simple guidelines are followed, the customer will usually feel appreciated and there is a high likelihood that the customer will return with an order of some kind. If these guidelines are abandoned, the customer may feel under-appreciated, misunderstood, or mistreated, in which case a return by that customer is highly unlikely.

Everyone needs to realize that the customer provides the lifeblood of the corporation. Without buying customers, there is no need for anyone to be employed. They, by their purchases, ensure employment and financial security. Hence, they must be treated with the respect and courtesy they deserve. This is true whether one works in a development or a retail environment. The conclusion is the same. The only difference is the cycle time and the financial magnitude of the purchases, but the impact is identical in either case.

All employees need to recognize this reality and act accordingly. Like it or not, we are dependent upon the good graces of our customers. Alienation of customers is highly undesirable and it is certainly counter-productive. As they say, it is like 'biting off one's own nose to spite one's face', or 'biting the hand that feeds you'. There is no productive point in doing that!

So, always treat one's customers with respect and consideration and all will end well.

Another useful point in interacting with customers is to never be condescending or patronizing. It does not come across well. Instead, it comes across as arrogant and generally unpleasant.

Sometimes it is necessary to re-educate a customer because he or she holds erroneous views. This is truly tricky to do. It is not an easy task. In re-educating a customer, one must find a way to be non-threatening, non-arrrogant and humble. It is tough to do, and yet make the necessary correction in the customer's understanding. The key here is the proper use of tact. This is usually learned. Some fortunate folks understand the use of tact from the 'getgo'. Others have to learn it.

Re-education, without tact, is usually counter-productive. If one is unfamiliar or uncomfortable with this approach, then perhaps it is best to assign another, more tactful person to do the re-education, so that the customer will welcome the new information instead of feeling 'put down' upon, defensive, ignorant or patronized.

In any event, the customer must be made to feel welcome and safe. He or she often needs to be re-assured. The final goal is to get the customer to 'buy'. The correct environment must be established by the employee to produce a positive interaction with the customer.

By following some of the guidelines presented here, the chance of success with prospective customers is very high. Remember: Nothing and no one is more important than the customer! If necessary, all other activities should be placed at the back of the line, rather than the customer, who belongs at the head of the line.

Customer service is paramount. In a development

environment, this means the provision of training courses, support engineering, manuals of operation, etc.

In a retail environment, it means helping the customer out in any reasonable sales-oriented way, such as showing a customer where a particular product or item may be located in the store, even if it is not within the employee's normal area of responsibility. This includes, but is not limited to, suggesting a layaway option when appropriate, carrying and loading heavy purchased objects into a customer's vehicle, helping a customer find a product, etc.

Bottom Line: A customer will usually return if he or she is treated with respect and consideration, and if that same customer is given first-class service and attention.

It is always best to attempt to help a customer by listening to the customer's needs, and by searching for a solution, even if one is not found. I have discovered that it is the intention rather than the result that matters most to a customer. The best outcome is when the customer's needs can be met and a solution found. In such a case, the satisfaction, on the part of the customer, is maximized. It is the intention and the attempt that is recognized most by a customer.

# Chapter Twelve:

# 'Leaders' Seek Out Initiators

# Not Complainers

More Thoughts On Leadership

## Chapter Twelve: 'Leaders' Seek Out Initiators, Not Complainers

Diligent problem-solvers and doers try to solve problems and present proposed solutions or already achieved solutions. No one wants to listen to incessant complaints or to constantly hear of problems and issues. Cassandra, the Greek prophetess of Doom, had few in her audience, probably because she spoke of nothing but negativity. So, complaints and a sense of forboding are usually unwelcomed in any environment.

Instead 'leaders' want to know of proposed or actualized solutions. After all, 'leaders' have more than enough to be concerned about on a daily basis. He or she does not wish to be constantly bombarded by complaints. Solutions are seen as a welcomed reprieve from this mournful chorus. The 'leader' may very well be and is often aware of any issues or problems that exist. He or she may have been assigned to solve these issues. They don't wish or need to be reminded constantly of their existence.

Usually, it is an easy thing to acknowledge and identify problems. It is quite another thing to find and implement real solutions to those very same problems. The latter takes a great deal of initiative, drive and imagination. The former requires neither.

Imagine yourself in a similar 'leadership' position. Which would you rather deal with?: a whiner and complainer or an initiator, who seeks to solve the very same set of issues or problems? The answer is indeed obvious and the initiator thereby becomes a much more valuable contributor to the entire 'team' or 'staff' effort and as a consequence, to the 'leader'.

It is even better if the solution has already been actualized, then even less effort is required because the problem is then a 'done deal', and the associated risks have been identified and have already been eliminated. No uncertainty remains. The 'leader' will most likely be relieved for this 'gift' from the initiator. This removes the need for the 'leader' to resolve this one additional issue.

As a consequence, the 'leader' is sure to recall the names of these very same initiators or self-starters when the next crisis approaches. This is not only good for the 'leader' but for those eventually aspiring to become 'leaders'. When the 'leader' finds people he or she can rely upon consistently to solve difficult and tricky problems. he or she can then develop a pre-identified cadre of problem-solvers that can always be relied upon, especially when the going gets really tough and rough.

Additionally, this cadre will already be

identified in the eyes of the 'leader' and his senior staff. This cannot be a bad thing for the people belonging to this unique and reliable group. By belonging and by being identified as a member of this special group, (s)he will stand out against all others team members who are not as motivated or diligent. In turn, this group is more likely to advance more quickly in management and the 'leadership' ranks. The reputations of the unofficial members will precede them since 'excellent' performers are often talked about in the upper ranks. They are known to take the initiative, to be creative and to be unafraid. These are essential characteristics of any great 'leader'.

Bottom Line: Never be afraid to 'act' when others 'recoil'. Be pro-active, rather than passive and accepting of mediocre results. Make positive change a part of yourself and your work ethic. Instead of whining and complaining, seek to solve the problem and then speak of how the overwhelming problem can be solved.

One cannot help but stand out when a long-standing issue is suddenly clarified and solved by someone who dares not to accept the on-going norm but chooses instead to recognize the problem and take the necesary initiative to solve it, especially when others either accept the norm or run away from problems. Be a problem-solver not a complainer.

# More Thoughts On Leadership

# Chapter Thirteen:

# Seek Always To Increase

# Team/Operational Efficiency

# More Thoughts On Leadership

# Chapter Thirteen: Seek Always To Increase Team/Operational Efficiency

Team efficiency and effectivity is a true reflection of the current 'leadership'. It is one of the 'leader's' job functions to ensure that each 'staff' member is working at full capacity and full capability. To do this, the 'leader' needs to always ensure that the necessary tools and supplies are made available to them as needed. Often there are existing tools, and new additional tools that may be better and allow even greater efficiency for a small initial outlay in cost. These should always be investigated on a 'break-even' analysis basis. In other words, not all tools are worthy of purchase because it may take too long for the resulting expected efficiency to produce the cost savings that match the initial cost expenditure. In general, given the caveats expressed above, better tools generally result in improved efficiency and efficacy, which make the bottom line easier to achieve, provided the cost of such tools does not outweigh their usefulness. Usually, better tool make the 'team' operate with minimal effort but with maximum efficiency and productivity. In this way, the overall objectives of the 'team' or 'staff' are most likely to succeed, and that is the ultimate goal, and the 'leader's' and/or the 'corporate's' main objective.

This chapter ellucidates the advantage of providing tha 'team' or 'staff' with the materials that are needed to perform a job function. This chapter is not about training, which is discussed in another chapter ('Training') of this book. In this chapter, the discussion is about materials, tools and applications, i.e. resources that allow an employee to properly function at his or her assigned task. This has been touvhed on in an earlier chapter nut it bears repoaeting in its own chapter.

If the 'team' or 'staff' cannot perform its task in the best, most effective way possible, it is not likely to meet the end goals. That is the 'leader's' job. There is no benefit in having the 'team' or 'staff' members daily search for ways around a given problem when a minor cost investment in material can make these useless efforts unnecessary and labor-intensive. The benefits of informal anfd formal training have already been discussed in the chapter on "Training" (Chapter 9

If the issue is never addressed adequately, the same unproductive effort is repeated over and over by each 'staff' member, to no avail. In the meantime, labor costs are being expended unnecessarily. This drives up the overall cost to do anything and reduces the profit potential of the company.

It is best to initially expend the small amount of material dollars and save a great deal of labor cost in the process. This will also improve 'staff' morale and allow more time to be made available for other, more profit-productive activities. Besides, the highest cost element in any activity is the labor cost. So, this should be reduced as much as possible.

If the environment is retail, this means more time is made available for customer interaction and possible sales, or for stocking and organization.

For development environments, it means that more time is made available for further testing, development, customer interaction, or corporate reporting.

In either case, it can unburden the 'staff' or 'team' member to pursue more productive and cost-effective activities. There is no loser in improving the efficiency of one's team. All can benefit, including the leader.

Bottom Line: Always provide the 'staff' or 'team' what is needed to perform its function. Never penny pinch on materials. Never be afraid to ask for any improvement suggestions from one's 'staff'. Encourage the 'staff' to identify such shortages or needed improvements. The 'leader' always has the last say, as he or she is ultimately held accountable for the overall performance. Subsequently, if a suggestion is a poor one, or is too costly, or is untimely, etc, the 'leader' can always decline the suggestion. There is no compulsion to follow-through with any suggestion.

In the end, the 'leader' must decide. In addition, only he or she can see the entire picture because of their overview of everything within their area of jurisdiction.

Enable one's 'staff'. That is how it should be.... always.

# More Thoughts On Leadership

# Chapter Fourteen:

## Title, Authority & Responsibilty

# More Thoughts On Leadership

# Chapter Fourteen: Title, Authority & Responsibility

Title, authority and responsibility usually go hand in hand. One without the others make the holder and the responsible person ineffective in the performance of his or her assigned task. An individual may possess a title without the associated respect. With the assigned title, the recipient may initially feel proud and distinguished. However, it will soon appear that the title is useless without the associated power, respect  and authority.

A title distinguishes a a particular 'staff' or 'team' person from the others, so that that individual will also be recognized as some kind of representative of the upper level 'leaders' and as an experienced individual worthy of the titled recognition. Otherwise, the title would never have been assigned. Hence, the title is necessary as an implicit indication by those at higher 'leadership'/management positions above. It also means that the designated individual is recognized as worthy, skilled, experienced and deserving of the title. The responsibilities of the new position are entrusted to the newly entitled individual, as part of his or her new job function.

But, to be effective in any role one must have commensurate  authority over others and the work they do. No worker will listen consistently to anyone who is merely titled, without that same authority to execute. Title and responsibility alone are insufficient. In other words, he or she must also be granted the 'power' or the 'authority'  to define the work of others, to reward and reprimand them, or to hire and fire employees for poor performance. Without such authority, staff member may not  listen, show the corrrect respect, or obey any commands.

On the other hand, authority without the corresponding title can also be detrimental. Such an untitled employee, who may have the authority and the responsibility but not the commensurate title, can only go so far in convincing others that what they are being commanded to do is indeed sanctioned by the high-level 'leaders'. In this case, there is no recognized or formally titled individual. He or she is acting without the proper tools to affect others, positively or negatively.  Title should carry with it unquestioned authority. Instead, lack of title carries with it ambiguity and uncertainty, causing the 'staff' to question the untitled authority.

He or she may be performing the job function but may not be seen as possessing the necessary title or job function recognition. There may have never been any formalization of the process. This can lead to mutiny, confusion and chaos. Some outspoken senior 'staff' members may not do anything until the issue is clarified.

Again, this is very negative for the 'team' or 'staff' effort and it is embarrassing to the people involved. The sooner these types of misshaps are clarified, the better for the 'team' or "staff' and the less embarrassment for anyone involved.

This is especially true when many of the projects are located overseas or are located distant from the central office. All team members need to know clearly who does and who does not have authority and responsibility. Formal recognition makes it very clear who to contact in any situation.

It clarifies and brings into clear focus who is in

charge of a given activity. It eliminates chaos so that forward movement on a project can result.

Along with responsibility and authority comes accountabilty. This is the least-liked aspect of any position because it means that the manager is held responsible for the 'staff's' share of the assigned effort and of his or her abiltiy to lead others.

Further, it is usually advisable to provide 'staff' with the materials it needs, in order for them to adequately perform their assigned function. This may mean something as simple as a computer, printer, display screen, pencils, pens, paper, binders, soap, tissue, mops, etc, depending upon the job. Being unable to do one's job because of resource shortages is simply unacceptable and the goals set out for the 'staff' are generally unachievable. This was discussed at some length in the previous chapter.

Respect usually must be earned or at least acknowledged by others because of previous experience. It usually does not come with the title. One, so titled, must have already won, up to that point, or may win the future respect of others by his or her performance at some point in time.

Of all the most difficult managerial transitions, the greatest transition is that from individual worker or contributor to that of a first-line supervisor or manager. The primary responsibility of the first position is as a direct contributor, with no real responsibility for the work output of others. In the supervisory position, one is responsible, for the first time, for the output of others under one's own direction. The emphasis changes from 'self' to 'others'. and to their work load. The emphasis becomes one of maximizing their efficiency, increasing the quality of their work, training, dealing with interpersonnal issues and conflicts, becoming a 'good' listener, learning and promulgating corporate rules and procedures, writing and evaluating performance and salary reviews, interpreting and distributing directives from top managemenet, etc. The emphasis is quite different and it requires a large adjustment.

Bottom Line: a position title without the commensurate authority, or having the proper authority without the commensurate position title are equally ineffective and cause an unnecessary drain on the 'team's' or 'staff's' bottom line.

It is best to award title, authority and responsibility, at the same time, so that chaos and confusion never start, at least not because of this.

Chapter Fifteen:

A Sense of Alacrity & Promptness

More Thoughts On Leadership

# Chapter Fifteen: A Sense of Alacrity, & Promptness

All staff should show a sense of alacrity and promptness in performing any task. Otherwise, the apparent sense becomes one of laziness, and lack of diligence. This is sensed not only by the 'leaders' and management but by customers too.

If the environment is a development one, then Requests For Proposals (RFPs) ought to be responded to promptly before or by the due date, regardless of when the RFP is received. In my own experience, government RFP's seemed to always appear just before the Christmas Holiday Season...not the best time to receive them. In addition, they were often due in the first week of January of the new calendar year. This was never truly appreciated by fellow associates because many of us had to work extra time through the Holiday Season, while the government customer had the time off. Nonetheless, as professionals, we also understood that this was the time to capture a new contract that would ultimately, along with several others, help to keep us all employed throughout the year. It was a Priority!

Frankly, at that time it was considered Priority Number One...nothing else mattered. It was a reality. None of us really enjoyed working long hours at that time of the year, especially when most everyone else, including the customer was starting to wind down, in preparartion for the upcoming Holiday Season. When it came down to it, we all realized that we really had no choice, like it or not. Had we done otherwise, some other 'hungrier' or 'more disciplined' contractor would have won the contract because ours would not have been submitted on time. Certainly, the 'late' RFP would not have even been considered.

Much the same is true in a retail environment. Sales can and often are lost to a customer because of a lack of any sense of neediness, or timeliness. There always needs to be a sense of alacrity and/or promptness. That is exactly how sales are lost. The customer can feel that his or her needs are not being addressed, much less heard.

Transfers from other store locations ought to be prompt and require no more than a week to complete. Corporate vehicles ought to be assigned on a 24-hour basis to ensure that customer's needs (transfer's, etc.) are processed and completed in a rapid, timely fashion...not in weeks but in days. Otherwise, that customer will lose patience and go to a more responsive competitor to satisfy his or her needs. In so doing, the sale will be lost.

The same is true of 'rain checks' or new orders. These ought to be processed as rapidly as possible. Furthermore, the data base ought to be checked daily to ensure that rapid response is the norm and the customer ought to be called by phone or e-mailed once the transferred or ordered item becomes available. Likewise, should any problem arise, the customer ought to be promptly informed of the new situation or problem, a solution proposed, and a new due date assigned. Only then will the waiting customer believe that his or her needs are being handled in the best possible way.

The real key to customer loyalty is service, service, service, in a timely manner. Any perceived lack of concern or urgency is the death knell with regard to that customer.

In addition, the 'leader', if he or she is alert, will perceive this lack of alacrity and take the appropriate internal correction steps and inform the customer of the situation.

This may require correction of a company system at the corporate level and so may require the support and action of higher management levels. If the action required involves the behavior of an employee, that employee needs to be informed of his or her inadequate action and corrective action taken by the supervisor or 'leader'. There is no need to do this publicly, but privately, as mentioned before in a previous chapter. The bottom line is affected in any case. So, correction of some kind is necessary.

Vengeance or punishment is not the final goal. It is the achievnment of the 'team', 'staff' and/or 'corporate' goals and objectives. It is also the ultimate satisfaction of the customer. Only by aligning the actions of all 'team' or 'staff' members and corporate sytems in this same direction, through the prompt addressing of customer needs, can this be achieved.

If it means dropping other tasks or subtasks to do so, then by all means do so. The customer will quickly see that addressing his or her needs first is the company priority and he or she will return with future business. And that will help to grow the bottom line, which is the desired result.

Bottom Line: Always demonstrate a sense of urgency in any action, especially any to do with a customer. A customer keeps everyone employed. Therefore his or her needs must be addressed promptly and in a timely manner, no matter what inconvenience that may produce for the employees. Remember, a customer can see all about him or her. The customer must always be assigned Priority One. A corporate system may need to be altered or an individual employee's behavior may need to be modified to achieve such a result.

# More Thoughts On Leadership

**Chapter Sixteen:**

**Neural Management**

More Thoughts On Leadership

# Chapter Sixteen: Neural Management

How can the organizational structure be modified and made to work for the 'leader'? This topic was introduced in the previous book but it will be discussed in more detail here, especially regarding neural management. .

Here we will talk specifically about 'neural' management, which is extremely horizontal in structure as opposed to the more common central management structure. This last structure is extremely bureaucratic, inefficient and slow to respond (because of the myriad levels of unnecessary bureaucracy). It is also very vertical in structure because of this.

It is my personal belief that responsibility and accountability should be pushed down to the lowest possible effective level, but accountability is paramount at each level. This is what I call neural management. It is efficient, empowering to the 'staff', quick in response and cost-effective.

Personally, I have seen this method work very successfully. It is the very opposite of central planning. It assumes a certain level of intelligence and good work ethic at the lower levels. It may not work in every instance, but when the staff can be counted upon to excel through their own efforts it can be very successful and very rewarding to 'staff'/'team' members, because they are by its nature 'empowered' to achieve results that benefit greatly the bottom line. The results can be truly amazing and in addition, it helps to create the next cadre of 'leaders'. It relieves the 'leader' of watching every little step, and frees him or her to watch the bigger picture more closely. It allows him or her to concentrate more on strategy and less on tactics. This can be done because more time is made available to the 'leader'. It reduces 'micromanagement'. But, and this is very important, such an approach only works with very intelligent and dedicated 'staff'. It requires a high level of confidence and trust in the 'staff' by the 'leader'.

It requires a certain amount of letting go of 'control' on the part of the 'leader'. This is not so easy when one is responsible for the output or the results of others. Handled incorrectly, or with the wrong 'staff' or 'team', this methodology can lead to disaster. However, with the right guidance, the right 'leader' and the right 'staff', this approach can produce wonders. However, it is not for everyone. Circumstances dictate whether this approach is the correct one to implement.

Also, this organizational structure builds team spirit because everyone now has a personal stake in the team performance. Useless and redundant middle level positions are eliminated, because all the decisions are made either directly below him or her, or if the decisions are strategic enough, above him or her, but at a reduced level of bureaucracy.

Should this structure and methodology be inmplemented however, under the right circumstances, the 'staff' can feel enabled and indeed 'empowered'. As mentioned before, the 'staff' closest to the task usually know more about the required functionality and any possible improvements that may be necessary than anyone.

Oftentimes, departments are allowed to grow to a size that outlives their usefulness. I believe that departments work best when they are smaller, when there exists a certain level of intimacy between the 'leader' and his or her staff. A smaller department often means better, closer, more intimate management, oversight and control of all activities and all employees within the purview of that 'leader' and that department or section.

As long as there is adequate 'staff' without an excess of it, there is usually less theft in such a department because there is always someone present who cares, giving thieves little chance to do their misdeeds. A smaller department is easier to staff. It eases reporting requirements and it can provide for more immediate and more useful feedback. It can provide greater visibility on problems and issues.

Bottom Line: Neural Organizational Structures can be empowering to the 'staff', productive, efficient and cost-effective. However, such a horizontal organizational structure can only work when the 'staff' is intelligent and dedicated. Otherwise, don't bother. Disaster will quickly follow.

Also, departments are often too large to operate effectively and efficiently. Usually, they will function more effectively if they are reduced in size.

Neural management and smaller department size can go hand-in-hand but they are also independent of each other. So, one can be implemented without feeling that the other must also be implemented. The overall goal is to better manage the bottom line. These methods, under the right circumstances, generally allow that.

# Chapter Seventeen:

# How Advertising & Sales

# Can Help Achieve Success

# (Retail Only)

# More Thoughts On Leadership

# Chapter Seventeen: How Advertising & Sales Can Help Achieve Success (Retail Only)

This chapter applies to the Retail environment and so the discussion will center around that topic. Advertising makes the customer aware of the company's presence. Without it, the customer may never become aware of the company's existence, its function, its services, its products, etc. Obviously, it is very important for a company to advertise for this reason, if no other.

Advertising entices a new customer to enter a previously unknown store. The customer might find that his or her curiosity is satisfied with the first visit, especially if a 'Sale' is underway in that store. Oftentimes, the customer may become quite excited by the prospects before him or her, especially if what the customer is seeking cannot be found elsewhere at that reduced 'Sale' price. The customer may also take note of the different items, services or products that are newly available to him or her.

Company Sales are a great way of doing just this: increasing awareness. The total revenue may increase but the profits may fall... momentarily only. The main benefit is that the customer will register the store in his or her memory banks for future use. That customer will most likely return when there is no Sale being held, and the profits will then recover. That is the whole point.

A store gets its profits from 'return customers' not from customers who may never return. This is one reason why customer service is so very important. It leaves a lasting impression or imprint on the customer's mind. Make that lasting impression a very positive and important one and that customer will be back for other items at a later time.

Advertising opens the door. Customer Service keeps the door open and holds it open for the customer. Advertising prompts the customer to act, in a way that is very favorable to the company. It gets the customer to check the place out, to get a proper feel for the place, its service mantra, its staff, its products, its location, etc. None of this can be a bad thing unless the service is very bad, products are out-of-stock, staff is rude and disrespectful, etc. If a product is out of stock, it is good customer relations to allow 'rain-checks' to be issued. That way, the customer does not feel that the company doesn't care about his or her needs, but that the company is merely out-of-stock at that moment because of unexpected high demand on a popular item. That, in itself, is a good sign to a customer, because he or she can see that the company normally stocks some very high demand, desirable products but it has been caught unaware by the unexpected high demand for the item due to the current 'Sale.

That will only cause the customer to return for other like items, especially if the customer receives a 'rain check' for the popular but out-of-stock item. If a 'rain check' is denied, the store more than likely will never see that customer again, because the customer will feel re-buffed and rejected, especially if the customer has come to the store to purchase the specific item for which the 'rain check' is being denied. In addition, the store can then be seen by the potential customer as untrustworthy and inconsistent in keeping its word about "Sale' items.

Sometimes, there is some confusion about on-line names and web-sites. This should be examined and corrected quickly because it too creates confusion and uncertainty. If the customer believes that he or she has seen that the product is either available or priced more lowly on a website, and that the website is mistakenly identified with the store because of similar naming or whatever, then there is nothing left but bad feeling and a sense of being 'taken advantage of'. The item in question appears to belong to the company but it does not. This can lead to confusion, chaos and consternation on the part of the customer. It reflects very negatively on the store. It appears that the store does not have its act together. The store appears very disorganized. It creates a negative shopping experience. The desire is to make the experience positive from the very start, not negative. Why engage in self-defeat when there are enough challenges to overcome each day without shooting oneself in the proverbial foot. This is very bad busines practice and it should be addressed and corrected at the earliest possible moment.

Bottom Line: Advertising and Company Sales are meant to introduce new customers to the store or to the company. Be sure that the customer experience is a positive enduring one via openness, responsivenesss, helpfulness, additional service, etc.

Remove any ambiguity about web-site names. This only causes customer confusion and alienation. In addition, upper management should always ensure that sufficient stock items are available, especally those that are 'On Sale'. Honor all items that have witnessed an unforeseen demand, with 'rain-checks' and the like.

NEVER leave your customer 'out in the cold'. It is a very poor business practice.

More Thoughts On Leadership

# Chapter Eighteen:

# Never Mislead Customers About Product Availability

# (Retail Only)

# Chapter Eighteen: Never Mislead Customers About Product Availability

## (Retail Only)

This may sound trivial but it can lead to customer confusion and disgruntlement. The staff who handles the front registers in a retail environment usually also answer or forward incoming telephone calls from enquiring customers. So far, so good. What if the customer lives some distance away from the store and he or she calls by telephone to enquire about the availabliity of a given product. If the employee answering an incoming telephone call from a potential customer, is really unfamiliar with the availability of a given product, then that call should be forwarded to someone in the particular department who is familiar with the current stock situation, or who can verify availability and pricing. Otherwise misinformation can be forwarded to the customer. This misinformation, may cause the customer to drive a great distance at great inconvenience and expense on the mistaken belief that a particular product is indeed available and on the shelf at a given store location. If the customer then pursues this mission to find that the store is actually 'out of stock' on that particular item, that customer is going to be very upset and may ask for the manager to sort out the situation.

Not only will the customer be rightly upset, but that same customer is likely never to return to that store and he or she may even 'bad mouth' the store to his or her friends

111

and family. Neither of these situations is a positive reflection on the store in question. It is the very opposite!

Bottom Line: It behooves the staff who answer incoming customer telephone calls, regarding availability of products, to defer these matters to the staff in the appropriate department. This avoids the aforementioned problem and off-loads the responsibility to a (hopefully) more knowledgeable individual. This reduces the likeliehood of such mishaps happening repeatedly. The end result is a pool of largely satisfied customers, who are less likely to become disgruntled and more likely to return to the store for future sales.

The profit and revenue line more than likely will reflect this positive happening and that is the overall objective.

# Chapter Nineteen:

## 'We'

## vs

## 'I'

# Chapter Nineteen: 'We' vs 'I'

The 'leader' should try never to display any indication of arrogance. It is extremely 'off-putting'. One way to ensure that one comes across as arrogant is to constantly talk about "I" when 'we' is much more appropriate. After all, the team accomplishments are exactly that, the accomplishments of the 'team', in its entirety and that includes the 'leader'. It is not just the accomplishment of the 'leader' alone, nor, is it the accomplishment of the 'team' or 'staff' alone. Each needs the other for success to be achieved. Without a 'good' 'team', a great 'leader' can accomplish nothing. Likewise, the reverse is also true. Without a great 'leader, a 'great' 'team' can also not accomplish much. The 'team' or the 'staff' is then 'leaderless' and blind. Therefore, is is always appropriate to give credit where credit is deservedly due: to both the 'team or 'staff' and the 'leader'. They accomplished great things working together. Any synergies that have occurred have done so because of the efforts of both the 'leader' and the 'team' or 'staff'.

A 'leader' should never fall into the 'trap' of accepting recognition for his or her efforts alone, ignoring the efforts of the personnel that helped to make it happen. A 'leader' should always try to refer to the accomplishments as a collective effort. In other words, use 'we' when referring to these achievements rather than 'I'. The latter sounds self-absorbed (which it is) and unnecessarily ego-centric. Credit should always be given to the key achievers because without them, their sacrifices and achievements, nothing good would have ever occurred, and the end goal would never have been accomplished.

Bottom Line: It is up to the 'leader' to be gracious and to recognize the reality that the 'leader' and the 'team' or 'staff' need each other to accomplish great things. One needs the other. It is a collective effort not the effort of a single individual that makes success possible. It is 'we' not 'I' and the 'leader' ought to be cornizant of that fact and speak accordingly when credit is being assigned, by higher management levels, for the achievement of often-difficult goals.

Do not let false ego get in the way. In giving recognition to the 'team' members, the 'leader' gets more respect and admiration from the 'team' for the 'leader's' honesty and integrity. With regard to the 'leader', arrogance is thereby dispelled from the perspective of the 'team' or 'staff' member.

Remember: it is usually 'we' not 'I'.

Accept this reality, embrace it and demonstrate it to others, especially to higher ranking management.

'We' not 'I' take oneslf out of the equation and recognizes the efforts and achievements of others.

It is really that simple!

# Chapter Twenty:

## Conclusion

# More Thoughts On Leadership

# Chapter Twenty: Conclusion

To sum up, a 'leader' has many responsibilities but he or she also has many tools at hand to influence and to lead his or her 'team' or 'staff' to success, whether it be in a development or a retail environment. There are other environments for which many of these tools still apply, but I will leave it to the reader to make that inference.

A 'leader' sets the example and provides the tools that empower his or her team to do their job most efficiently and most effectively. However, the 'leader' must also be organized himself or herself in order to be truly effective. The points made in this book reinforce and add to the points made in the previous book, ***Thoughts on Leadership.***

A 'leader' is effective only if his or her 'team' is effective. A good 'team' needs a effective 'leader' and an effective 'leader' needs an intelligent and motivated 'team'. They need each other. One cannot succeed without the other.

The effective 'leader' must not only possess and practice all the qualities described in the first book, he or she must be a fair, honest and compassionate individual. He or she must be willing and open to the concept of 'listening' to 'team' and 'staff' members. Fairness is paramount, as are mutual respect and self-integrity. Be 'firm but fair'.

Some selected chapters apply only to the retail environment and may not be necessary in a development environment. The reader is left to decide what chapters pertain or do not pertain to his or her specific situation.

I have tried in these two companion books to pass on what I have learned and what I know. These are not, nor are they meant to be, theoretical books. Instead, the slant is very pragmatic, and based upon actual experience.

I hope the reader finds these discussions useful to the attainment of his or her corporate project and team goals.

***About The Author:*** John P. McWilliams, has worked at five different engineering development companies over the past 38 years. He started at a large defense contractor, in Wayland, MA, and continued on to work at several Silicon Valley 'Hi-tech' development companies.

He has designed and managed the development of radar, radar warning and telecommunications equipment. He has obtained a wealth of experience in both the design and the management of development projects for the U. S. and foreign governments.

He grew from engineer to task manager to project manager, to the positions of Department Manager for Programs & Systems Development to his final position as MSD (Multichannel Systems Division) Director of Programs (projects), at his final place of employment...a high-tech, Silicon Valley company.

As a project manager, he has personally managed more than one dozen projects of all contract types and he was approached numerous times by department managers, program managers and company founders to 'fix' broken (i.e. 'failing') projects. In each case, Mr. McWilliams, together with great technical 'teams', achieved success and turned problem projects around.

Because of his success in managing many complex, difficult projects, sometimes simultaneously, he became the department manager for Programs & Systems Development at the last company he worked for. Later, in the same company, he was awarded the position of MSD Programs Director, wherein, he was responsible for setting project and design standards, and for overseeing more than 50 projects each month, over four states with a combined yearly revenue of approximately $75 million.

He retired to New Mexico in 2007, where he now writes both fiction and non-fiction books. He formed two companies: Bria Ventures LLC  and Apache Management Consulting LLC.

The first company is related to his non-management writing of fiction, non-fiction, poetry and memoirs of his younger days in Scotland (where he was raised until he was nearly ten years of age) and the Bronx. He also performs free-lance writing assignments through Bria Ventures, LLC. The second company deals with management consulting and training topics.

He is a member of: National Association of Distinguished Professionals, National Professionals of Excellence and he is a Life Member of the Institute of Electrical and Electronic Engineers. He is also associated with five historical societies, and several southwestern writers' organizations.

He has published numerous non-fiction and fiction books. He has also written and published several memoirs and books with poetic content. He has written numerous newspaper and magazine articles, and he has presented six lectures on Apache Warrior Woman, Lozen.

He has crafted numerous management/leadership

MS Power Point presentations for his management company. This is his second book on the topic of Leadership and Management.

Since his Retirement in 2007, he has gained experience in the Retail space. Much of that experience is reflected in these pages. Although much is similar, there are unique differences between the two environments. Both the points of similarity and the differences are pointed out in these books.

www.ingramcontent.com/pod-product-compliance
Lightning Source LLC
Chambersburg PA
CBHW071445180526
45170CB00001B/468